A No... ...chers

DK READERS is a compelling reading programme for children. The programme is designed in conjunction with leading literacy experts, including Cliff Moon M.Ed., who has spent many years as a teacher and teacher educator specializing in reading. Cliff Moon has written more than 160 books for children and teachers. He is series editor to Collins Big Cat.

Beautiful illustrations and superb full-colour photographs combine with engaging, easy-to-read stories to offer a fresh approach to each subject in the series. Each DK READER is guaranteed to capture a child's interest while developing his or her reading skills, general knowledge, and love of reading.

The five levels of DK READERS are aimed at different reading abilities, enabling you to choose the books that are exactly right for your child:

Pre-level 1: Learning to read
Level 1: Beginning to read
Level 2: Beginning to read alone
Level 3: Reading alone
Level 4: Proficient readers

The "normal" age at which a child begins to read can be anywhere from three to eight years old. Adult participation through the lower levels is very helpful for providing encouragement, discussing storylines and sounding out unfamiliar words.

No matter which level you select, you can be sure that you are helping your child learn to read, then read to learn!

DK

LONDON, NEW YORK, MUNICH,
MELBOURNE, and DELHI

Editor Dawn Sirett
Art Editor Jane Horne
Series Editor Deborah Lock
Art Director Martin Wilson
Production Editor Sarah Isle
Picture Researcher Angela Anderson
Jacket Designer Natalie Godwin
Natural History Consultant
Theresa Greenaway

Reading Consultant
Cliff Moon, M.Ed.

First published in Great Britain by
Dorling Kindersley Limited
80 Strand, London WC2R 0RL

Copyright © 2000 Dorling Kindersley Limited
A Penguin Company
This edition 2012

10 9 8 7 6 5 4 3 2 1
001-185909-February 2012

A CIP catalogue record for this book
is available from the British Library

ISBN: 978-1-40539-336-2

Printed and bound in China by L Rex Printing Co., Ltd.

The publisher would like to thank the following for their kind
permission to reproduce their photographs:
a=above, b=below/bottom, c=centre, l=left, r=right, t=top

Ardea London Ltd: Peter Steyn 4 bl; **Bruce Coleman Collection Ltd**:
Trevor Barrett 6–7, 19 c, Erwin & Peggy Bauer 28,
Fred Bruemmer 10 t, Alain Compost front cover, 17,
Peter Davey 26 b, Chrisler Fredriksson 27 cl, 32 crb, Janos Jurka 22 t,
Steven C. Kaufman 15 t, 15 cr, 32 bl, Gunter Kohler 16 c,
Stephen Krasemann 24 b, Leonard Lee 7 t, Joe McDonald 3 b, 23 b,
M. R. Phicton 4 cra, 4 cr, Jorg & Petra Wegner 5 b; **NHPA**: B. & C.

www.dk.com

DK READERS

BEGINNING TO READ 1

Wild
Baby Animals

Written by Karen Wallace

A Dorling Kindersley Book

Animals grow up in different ways.
They have lots of lessons to learn.
Some are born helpless but
their mothers protect them.
A newborn kangaroo is the size
of a bee.

She crawls
into her
mother's
safe pouch.

She doesn't open her eyes
for at least five months.

A newborn monkey cannot walk.
He is carried by his mother.

Other baby animals
can walk soon after they're born.
They learn to run
with their mother
when danger is near.

Baby rhinos stand on their hooves
a few minutes after
they are born.

hooves

A baby zebra can run
an hour after she is born.

Some baby animals are born
in a place that is safe.
Other baby animals are born
in the open.

Baby wolves are born in a cave.

A baby elephant is born
on open, grassy land.

Other elephants
make a circle
to protect her.

All the animals in this book
drink their mother's milk.
They are called mammals.

A seal's milk is fatty and rich.
Baby seals need lots of fat
to keep warm in the snow.

Baby bears
suck milk
for six months.

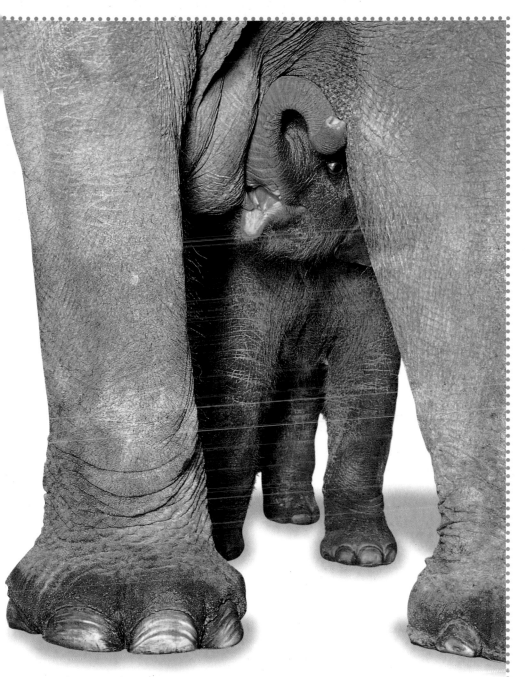

Baby elephants suck milk
for two years or more!

All baby mammals
stay by their mother
to keep safe.

On land, a baby walrus
stays tucked under her mother.

A baby kangaroo is carried
in his mother's pouch.

A baby sloth has to hold on tight.
Her mother is upside down!

Baby animals
must stay clean
to be healthy.

tongue

A mother cheetah
licks her cub's soft fur
with her rough tongue.

A monkey picks lice
from her baby's back
with her long fingers.

As baby animals grow
they need solid food.

Lion cubs eat
what their mother can catch.

Baby orang-utans
eat fruit
that their mother
has chewed for them.

Other baby animals
soon find food for themselves.
A baby buffalo eats grass.

A baby giraffe tears off leaves
with her thick lips.

Baby animals
know their mother's voice.
They find her quickly
if danger is near.

A baby dolphin
hears her mother
make a click-click-click sound.

CLICK!
CLICK!
CLICK!

A baby seal
knows her mother's bark. ARRK!

When there's danger in the water, baby animals do as they're told.

Baby beavers dive
when they hear
the whack
of their
mother's tail.

tail

A baby hippo
stays with his mother
when she grunts a loud warning.

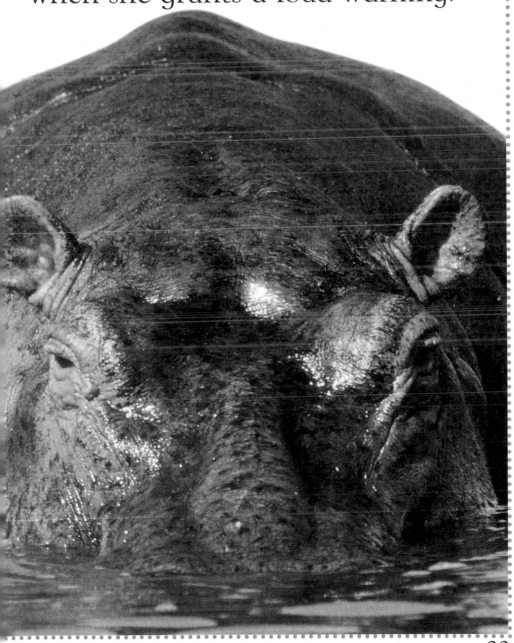

When there's danger
in the forest,
baby animals do as they're told.

A fawn lies still
in the grass
so she won't be seen.

Bear cubs
climb a tree
when their
mother growls.

As baby animals grow older
they start
to look after themselves.

A young chimpanzee
uses a stick to dig for insects.

Otter cubs learn to swim
so they can
catch fish.

trunk

A young elephant
uses her trunk
to rip leaves
from a tree.

Baby animals play games
that teach them how
to look after themselves.

Wolf cubs wrestle and bite.
They're pretending to hunt.

Baby koalas play in the trees.
They're learning to climb
with their sharp claws.

claws

Baby animals grow up.
They learn their lessons well
and no longer need
their mothers.

Koalas are
fully grown
at two years.

Elephants are
fully grown
at twenty-five!

One day baby animals
are old enough
to have babies of their own.

Glossary

Claws
sharp nails on the end of an animal's hand or toes

Hooves
a horned covering over the foot of an animal

Tail
a movable body part joined to an animal's bottom

Tongue
a fleshy part in the mouth used for tasting and eating

Trunk
the long nose of an elephant